Whe

RECIPE BOOK

Simple, nutritious ideas for
the whole family using SOLGAR *Whey to Go®*
Protein Powder.

———————

WRITTEN BY
Alice Bradshaw D.N. MED

RECIPES BY
Alice Bradshaw D.N. MED
Christine Bailey MSc PGCE

PUBLISHED BY
Solgar UK [LTD]

First published in Great Britain in 2009 by
Solgar UK [LTD], Aldbury, Hertfordshire, HP23 5PT

ISBN 978-0-9563537-1-9

Printed and bound by Burlington Press

RECIPE NOTES
Both Metric and Imperial measurements are given for the recipes.

This book includes dishes made with nuts and nut derivatives.

All the recipes in this book have been analysed by a professional
nutritionist. The analysis refers to each serving.

Contents

4 Solgar *Whey to Go*® Protein Powder

6 All about Protein

10 Whey Protein and your health

14 Cooking with Whey Protein

15 Healthy ingredients

21 *Whey of Life* recipe index

23 Smoothies and Shakes

35 Breakfast dishes

45 Savoury dishes

55 Muffins

63 Flapjacks, bars and sweet treats

77 Desserts

Solgar *Whey to Go*® Protein Powder

THE HEALTH-PROMOTING ASSETS of whey have been appreciated for centuries. According to an expression from Florence, Italy, circa 1650, *"Chi vuol viver sano e lesto beve scotta e cena presto" (If you want to live a healthy and active life, drink whey and dine early)*.

Although traditionally seen as a food for athletes and sports people, more and more people are starting to recognise the value of Whey Protein. From children to seniors, the whole family can take advantage of this tasty natural food.

SOLGAR *Whey to Go*® Protein Powder is an all-natural milk-derived, high-quality protein source that is lactose-free and low in fat and calories. It is free of cholesterol, artificial flavours and sweeteners, salt and starch. Additionally, it is manufactured from cows not treated with rBGH, [recombinant bovine growth hormone].

Whey to Go® Protein Powder is available in four delicious flavours:

- Natural Vanilla Bean flavour
- Natural Chocolate Cocoa Bean flavour
- Natural Honey Nut flavour
- Natural Mixed Berry flavour

Whey Protein Powder is a delicious and versatile ingredient that can be used to enhance the nutritional value of many dishes. It can be incorporated into smoothies, pancakes, muffins and even main dishes.

WHEY TO GO®
FOR YOUR WHEY OF LIFE

- Great source of protein
- Easy to mix and tastes great
- Low in fat and calories
- Lactose-free
- Derived from cows not treated with growth hormone

FOR MORE INFORMATION VISIT
www.solgar-vitamins.co.uk

SOLGAR VITAMINS | essentials for life's journey

All about Protein

Why do I need protein?

Protein is a macronutrient required by everyone on a daily basis. It is made up of amino acids, which are known as the building blocks for a healthy body. The main roles of protein include:

- Formation and repair of body cells including: tissue, muscles, bones, hair, skin and nails
- Manufacturing of enzymes
- Manufacturing of hormones
- Maintenance of immune health
- Provides a source of energy

Which foods are good sources of protein?

Protein is found in many foods, but particularly rich sources include eggs, dairy products, meat and fish. Pulses, nuts and seeds provide good vegetarian sources of protein.

Food	Portion Size	Protein [g]
Chicken	1 breast	39
Turkey, light meat	2 slices 140g	47
Cod, poached	1 fillet 120g	25
Tuna canned in brine	1 small tin 100g	24
Cheese, cheddar	1 thick slice 40g	10
Low fat yogurt, plain	1 carton 150g	6
Eggs	1, size 2	8
Cashew nuts	1 handful 50g	10
Walnuts	1 handful 50g	7
Baked beans	1 small tin 205g	10
Red lentils	3 tbsp 120g	9
Chick peas	3 tbsp 140g	12
Tofu [soya bean curd]	Half a pack 100g	8

How much protein do I need?

The amount of protein needed daily for good health is a
hotly debated topic in the nutrition world. The
government has set the recommended dietary allowance
[RDA] as 0.8g protein per kilogram body weight. So for
example, a woman weighing 57kg [9 stone] would require
46g of protein daily. Most experts in nutrition believe that
this level is too low, especially for active individuals
and those with special requirements, such as pregnant
women, the elderly, or infirm. Taking into account
individual differences, such as age, weight and gender, the
Institute of Medicine [IOM] recommends that we all aim to
obtain 10-35% of our total calories from protein.

FOR A MAN consuming the recommended 2500 Calories a day, this equates to 62-220 g of protein daily.

FOR A WOMAN consuming the recommended 2000 Calories a day, this equates to 50-175 g of protein daily.

What is Whey Protein?

Whey Protein is a naturally occurring derivative of the cheese-making process [remember little Miss Muffet eating her 'curds and whey'?]. Whey naturally contains a small amount of fat and some minerals, but is predominantly composed of a high-quality protein containing smaller protein sub-fractions and minor peptides – all with amazing health-promoting properties. Modern technology has allowed for the isolation of the active protein sub-fractions and various other components, while removing fat and lactose from the whey. The result is a high-quality protein supplement that is versatile and delicious.

How does Whey Protein compare to other protein sources?

Whey Protein is a high-quality, complete protein with rich amounts of all the essential amino acids [building blocks of protein]. Biological Value [BV] is a measure of how efficiently protein is used in the body. Whey is thought to have the highest biological value compared to all protein sources, including eggs and red meat.

Can I use *Whey to Go*® Protein Powder if I have intolerance to dairy foods?

Possibly. Most people who cannot tolerate dairy products actually have either lactose intolerance or are sensitive to casein, which is a milk protein. The highly efficient ion exchange and microfiltration processes used in the manufacturing of *Whey to Go*® removes all but trace amounts of casein and completely removes lactose. Therefore some people may well be able to use *Whey To Go*®, even if they cannot tolerate most dairy products. Furthermore, whey has been shown to be an easily digested form of protein suitable for even more sensitive individuals.

Studies show that Whey Protein Powder may help to improve whole body wellness by supporting healthy weight, immune health and the ageing process.

Research on the health benefits of whey has been carried out in the following areas:

- Weight management
- Ageing
- Sports nutrition
- Cardiovascular health
- Immune health

Whey Protein
and your health

Whey Protein and immune health

Our ability to stay well and fight off illnesses and poor health is largely dependent on a strong immune system.

Whey Protein supports optimal immune health by replenishing the body's levels of glutathione, an important immune-regulating compound found in the cells of the body. Low levels of glutathione are associated with poor health.

Whey Protein also contains other naturally occurring immune-supportive compounds, including lactalbumin and immunoglobulin.

HORTON BS. Commercial utilization of minor milk components in the health and health food industries. *J Dairy Sci*, 1995.78 [11] p.2584-9

Whey Protein and ageing

As the human body ages, changes in body composition and metabolism are almost inevitable. Factors such as dietary changes and a reduction in physical activity contribute to these changes, but the ageing process by its very nature is the main contributor. Physical activity and a diet containing an adequate level of high-quality proteins can help to ward off the debilitating muscle loss [and fat gain] commonly associated with ageing.

Whey is a practical addition to the diet of the more mature adult, as high-quality protein is essential for the maintenance of muscle tissue, organs and proper metabolism.

DOHERTY TJ. Invited review: Aging and sarcopenia. *J Appl Physiol*, 2003. 95[4]: p.1717-27

Whey Protein and weight management

Whey Protein is a valuable tool to those looking to reduce their body fat levels and manage their overall body weight. Protein has appetite-suppressing and blood-sugar-stabilising properties and in studies, people given a whey drink before a meal felt less hungry when consuming fewer calories. The studies show that whey stimulates two appetite-regulating hormones that are found in the gut. In addition, Whey Protein helps to preserve valuable lean tissue [muscle] which is vital for supporting healthy metabolism and fat loss.

HALL WL, MILLWARD DI *et al*. Casein and whey exert different effects on plasma amino acid profiles, gastrointestinal hormone secretion and appetite. *Brit J Nutr.* 89, 239-248, 2003

Whey Protein and cardiovascular health

Coronary heart disease is a leading cause of poor health in Western society. Research has consistently shown that diet plays a pivotal role in heart health and Whey Protein contains certain compounds [known as bioactive peptides] that may have a positive effect on cardiovascular health.

SHARPE S, GAMBLE G, SHARPE D, 1994. "Cholesterol-lowering and blood pressure effect of immune milk." *American Journal of Clinical Nutrition*, 59:929-934.

AS PART OF A HEALTHY, BALANCED DIET, WHEY PROTEIN
IS A VALUABLE ADDITION FOR ANYONE INTERESTED IN
OPTIMAL HEALTH.

Whey Protein and bone health

Bone is an active living tissue and requires various
nutrients to keep it in good health. Although calcium is
considered the chief bone nutrient, the role of protein in
bone health is often overlooked. Protein stimulates the
production of certain growth factors involved in bone
formation. Although there is concern over excess protein
and calcium depletion, recent studies have demonstrated
that adequate protein and calcium almost certainly work
synergistically to improve bone mass. Exciting new
research even suggests that Whey Protein may enhance the
development of bone forming cells known as osteoblasts.

HANNAN, M. *et al.*, 2000. "Effect of dietary protein on bone loss in
elderly men and women: The Framingham Osteoporosis Study."
Journal of Bone & Mineral Research, 15[12]:2504-2512.

Whey Protein in sports nutrition

Perhaps the best known use for Whey Protein is its role as
a key constituent in the diet of sportsmen and women and
people who generally like to keep fit and active. The
popularity of whey among athletes has much to do with
the benefits related to body composition [increased lean
muscle and enhanced fat reduction], but there are other
benefits. For athletes engaged in weight-lifting and other
anaerobic sports, the ingestion of Whey Protein after

training is associated with quicker recovery and improvements in strength. Interestingly, the amino acid profile of whey is almost identical to that of skeletal muscle.

LEMON, W.R. *et al*, 1996. "Is increased dietary protein necessary or beneficial for individuals with a physically active lifestyle?" *Nutrition Reviews Supplement*, 54:S169-175.

Whey for the whole family

Whey Protein is a great addition for anyone interested in good health. When incorporated into meals, whey protein is suitable for young and old alike. Children can benefit from the healthy properties found in whey and will enjoy the smoothies, muffins and other treats featured in this recipe book. Whey Protein is similar in structure to the basic proteins found in breast milk, and most infant feeding formulae are whey based. So children, adults and the elderly can all enjoy the tasty and health-promoting properties of Whey Protein Powder.

JOST, R. *et al.*, 1999. "Aspects of whey protein usage in infant nutrition, a brief review." *International Journal of Food Science and Technology*, 34:533-542.

Cooking with Whey Protein

THE VERSATILITY of Whey Protein makes it a simple ingredient to work with. Typically, it is incorporated into smoothies and shakes, however there are many more quick and easy ways to add whey to your diet.

Whey Protein can be added to savoury dishes and used as an ingredient in bakes, muffins, and healthy snacks. Many of the recipes using Whey Protein can be conveniently packed into a child's lunchbox or transported easily to eat mid-morning at your office desk.

Whey Protein Powder lends itself especially well as a breakfast ingredient. Smoothies and shakes are popular morning choices, but opting for pancakes, muffins and cereal bars are also great ways of adding more whey to your morning meal.

Whey Protein Powder blends easily with other ingredients. For baked goods, just add it to the other dry ingredients [flours etc].

These tried and tested recipes are firm favourites among Whey Protein users and will encourage you to experiment more with this exciting ingredient.

Healthy ingredients

THE SECRET to a healthy recipe is to choose your ingredients wisely. Independent health food stores now contain an array of ingredients that offer a wholesome alternative to ingredients such as sugar or margarine.

Additionally, if you are on a special diet and needing to avoid foods such as wheat, gluten or milk, you will be able to find ingredients that support your dietary requirements and allow you to enjoy a rich and varied diet. Many of the recipes in this book can be adapted to meet the needs of those on restricted diets. Simply using non-dairy milk will make a recipe lactose-free and substituting wheat flour for one of the many wheat-free/gluten-free grain alternatives is also a practical option.

Agave nectar
Sometimes called agave syrup, agave nectar is a natural sweetener with a low glycemic index. It is made from the wild agave plant and can be used as a substitute to honey or golden syrup.

Baking powder
Gluten-free versions are available, using rice or potato flour rather than wheat.

Buckwheat
Often mistaken for a grain, buckwheat is a nutrient-rich, high-protein fruit seed. Ground into flour, it is a gluten-free alternative, popularly used in pancakes and waffles.

Buckwheat contains all eight essential amino acids, bioflavonoids, fibre and is an especially rich source of magnesium.

Chocolate – minimum 70% cocoa solids

The health benefits of cocoa can be obtained from a bar that contains at least 70% cocoa solids. Rich in magnesium, potassium and antioxidants, cocoa rich chocolate has a smooth velvety taste and is less sweet than commercial confectionary. The higher the concentration of cocoa solids, the more intense the cocoa flavour.

Coconut butter

Coconut butter is a versatile fat and perfect for cooking with. Although a saturated fat, coconut fat does not raise cholesterol levels and is a rich source of medium chain triglycerides [important fatty acids which are involved in energy production].

Eggs

Always choose organic [or at least free-range] eggs. Even better choose omega-3-enriched eggs.

Flaxseeds [ground]

Ground flaxseeds [also known as linseeds] add a nutty flavour to any sweet or savoury dish. They are an extremely rich source of healthy fats and fibre and will boost the nutrient content of any recipe.

Millet

A tiny bead-shaped grain that is perfect as an alternative for wheat-and gluten-free diets. It is a good source of protein, magnesium and B vitamins and has a high fibre content. Millet is available as a grain and as flakes. The flakes can be used as a substitute for oats to make a recipe gluten-free.

Nut butter

Unsalted nut butters, such as almond or cashew butter are great healthy store cupboard ingredients. A good source of essential fats, they can be used simply as spreads or incorporated into recipes.

Nut and seed milks

Almond and hazelnut milks are sweet-tasting alternatives to dairy or soy milks and are easily found in health-food shops. They can be used in cooking, and lend themselves especially well to baked goods.

Oats

Oats are a versatile healthy cereal grain. They are a rich source of many nutrients and are particularly rich in magnesium and soluble fibre. They can be utilised as an integral part of many recipes, as well as being eaten on their own as porridge.

Olive oil

A healthy monounsaturated oil – a source of omega 9 fatty acids and great for cooking with. Olive oil can be used in place of butter or other fats in many recipes.

Omega advanced blend 2:1:1
This oil is a rich source of the health-promoting essential fatty acids, omega 3 and 6, as well as omega 9, and can be added to smoothies, cold dishes and foods that have already been cooked.

Potato flour
A starch-rich flour, great as a thickener or as part of a combination of flours for gluten-free recipes.

Pure spread
Pure spreads are available in three varieties. These are a healthy alternative to margarine [containing no hydrogenated fats or GM ingredients] and are suitable for home cooking and baking. Choose from Pure Sunflower, Pure Soya or Pure Organic.

Quinoa
Pronounced *keen-wah*, this grain is a staple of the ancient peoples of Peru, where it is known as the 'mother grain'. Quinoa contains more protein than any other grain and is completely gluten-free. Quinoa is also available as a flour, as flakes or even as a milk alternative.

Rice flour
Rice flour can be used in sweet and savoury dishes. It works well combined with other gluten-free flours as an alternative to wheat flour. Rice flour is also great for thickening sauces.

Rice milk

As an alternative to cows' milk, rice milk has a mild sweet flavour and the consistency of skimmed milk. It can be used in any recipe where milk is required and the vanilla-flavoured rice milk works well in sweet dishes.

Silken tofu and soy yogurt

These are versatile foods made from soy beans. They can be used in any recipe as a substitute for dairy yogurt.

Soy milk

An alternative to dairy milk. Soy milk is available sweetened [with apple juice] or unsweetened, and even calcium-enriched. Use wherever milk is called for in a recipe.

Xantham gum

Pronounced zantham gum, this is a type of starch produced via fermentation [using corn]. It has the characteristics of being very stretchy, which makes it a useful substitute for gluten when baking breads, pastry or muffins.

Xylitol

Xylitol is a natural sweetener occurring in berries, fruit and vegetables. It is as sweet as ordinary sugar, yet has 40% fewer calories. It is tooth-friendly and low GI, which makes it a great choice as a sweetener for weight-management programmes. It can be used as a direct replacement for sugar in any recipe.

Whey of Life
Recipe index

23 **Smoothies and Shakes**

35 **Breakfast dishes**

45 **Savoury dishes**

55 **Muffins**

63 **Flapjacks, Bars and Sweet Treats**

77 **Desserts**

WHEY OF LIFE

Smoothies and Shakes

Simple Shakes

For a speedy, simple protein shake, combine any flavour of SOLGAR *Whey to Go® Protein Powder* with a glass of milk, milk alternative or fruit juice. Here are a few quick and easy ideas to get you inspired:

Vanilla Sunrise

This shake combines the fresh sweetness of orange juice with the delicate flavour of vanilla. Uniquely delicious.

300 ml / 10 oz fresh orange juice
1 scoop Solgar *Whey to Go® Powder* Vanilla flavour

Blend ingredients together and serve in a tall glass

Serves 1

NUTRITIONAL INFORMATION PER SERVING:
Calories 212, Fat 0.4g, Saturated fat 0.21g, Carbohydrates 31g, Fibre 0g, Protein 16g

Chocolate milk-shake

A classic recipe with a healthy twist.

Using chilled, sweetened soy milk gives the shake a smooth and creamy texture. This can also be heated and served as a delicious hot chocolate.

300 ml / 10 oz soy milk or other milk
1 scoop Solgar *Whey to Go® Protein Powder* Chocolate flavour

Blend ingredients together and serve in a tall glass

Serves 1

NUTRITIONAL INFORMATION PER SERVING:
Calories 235, Fat 7g, Saturated fat 1.4g, Carbohydrates 17.3g, Fibre 3.4g, Protein 27.1g

Double Vanilla Dream

A light, sweet aromatic drink – great served chilled with ice cubes. Superbly refreshing for a hot summer's day.

300 ml / 10 oz Vanilla Rice Milk
1 scoop Solgar *Whey to Go® Protein Powder* Vanilla flavour

Blend ingredients together and serve with ice

Serves 1

NUTRITIONAL INFORMATION PER SERVING:
Calories 223.5 Fat 3.4g, Saturated fat 0.21g, Carbohydrates 11g, Fibre 0g, Protein 17.5g

Banana Chilly Billy

This is a firm favourite, especially with children. Using frozen banana creates a thick creamy consistency, much like ice cream. Vary the amount of liquid used to achieve a consistency of your choice.

1 large banana, peeled, chopped and frozen for at least 3 hours [preferably over night]
200 ml / 7 oz water
1 scoop Solgar *Whey to Go® Protein Powder* Vanilla flavour

Blend ingredients together until smooth and serve in a tall glass

Serves 1

NUTRITIONAL INFORMATION PER SERVING:
Calories 182, Fat 0.4g, Saturated fat 0.21g, Carbohydrates 28g, Fibre 3g, Protein 17.1g

Black Forest

This traditional combination of chocolate and berries is a quick shake that also can be served as a light dessert-drink.

100 g / 4 oz fresh or frozen black forest fruits [or a combination of dark berries and cherries]
1 scoop Solgar *Whey to Go® Protein Powder* – Chocolate flavour
1 tsp xylitol [optional]
Approximately 200 ml / 7 oz water

Blend all ingredients together until smooth and serve in a tall glass

Serves 1

NUTRITIONAL INFORMATION PER SERVING:
Calories 179, Fat 2g, Saturated fat 0.5g, Carbohydrates 27g, Fibre 5g, Protein 17g

Super Smoothies

THESE NUTRITIOUS smoothies are more substantial than the simple protein shakes. They contain some whole-food ingredients or a selection of fruits and can be served as a meal [such as breakfast] as well as a substantial energy snack. They are simple to make and you can add your own twist to any of the recipes by varying the ingredients to your personal preferences. You can choose to use milk or a dairy alternative, or even just water is fine. You can even add minimal liquid and achieve a really thick smoothie that you can eat with a spoon.

Banana Beauty Boost

This sweet nutty smoothie contains essential fats, protein, vitamin E, magnesium, fibre and potassium – nutrients that promote healthy skin, nails and hair. Served thick, this makes a great breakfast.

1 banana [chopped and frozen – optional]
1 tbsp almond butter
1 scoop Solgar *Whey to Go*® *Protein Powder* –
Honey Nut flavour
1 tsp Solgar *Omega Advanced Blend 2:1:1*
½ tbsp ground flaxseeds
1 tbsp oatbran / oats / wheatgerm [optional]
Water – enough to create the desired consistency

Blend all ingredients together and serve immediately

Serves 1

NUTRITIONAL INFORMATION PER SERVING:
Calories 379, Fat 13.9g, Saturated fat 0.81g, Carbohydrates 41.5g,
Fibre 7.1g, protein 21.3g

Mango Madness

The sweet perfume of luscious mangoes combined
with carrot juice makes for a surprisingly delicious and
nutritious smoothie.

1 ripe mango
1 ripe banana [chopped and frozen for at least 3 hours]
240 ml / 8oz carrot juice
2 scoops Solgar *Whey to Go® Protein Powder*
Vanilla flavour
1 tsp *Omega Advanced Blend 2:1:1* [optional]
1 tbsp ground flaxseeds
8 tbsp live natural yogurt

Blend all ingredients until smooth and serve in tall glasses

Serves 2

NUTRITIONAL INFORMATION PER SERVING:
Calories 367.5 Fat 10.1g , Saturated fat 2.5g, Carbohydrates 44.2g,
Fibre 5.8g, Protein 25.4g

Berry Sensation

A great summer smoothie making use of seasonal berries.
Can also be made out of season with frozen berries.

6 strawberries
1 large handful of blueberries
5 blackberries
180 ml / 6 oz rice / soy / dairy milk or water
1 scoop Solgar *Whey to Go® Protein Powder* –
Mixed Berry flavour
1 tsp *Omega Advanced Blend* [optional]

Blend all ingredients together until smooth and serve
in a tall glass

Serves 1

NUTRITIONAL INFORMATION PER SERVING:
Calories 230, Fat 5.5g, Saturated fat 0.5g, Carbohydrates 26g,
Fibre 4.5g Protein 16g

Tropical Digestive Delight

Packed with fibre, probiotics and enzymes, this light and creamy smoothie contains natural ingredients that are known to support digestive health.

1 papaya
8 oz fresh pineapple
2 sticks of Solgar *Caricol Organic Papaya Fruit Puree*
8 tbsp live natural yogurt
2 tbsp ground flaxseed
2 scoops Solgar *Whey to Go® Protein Powder*
Vanilla flavour
½ tsp grated ginger [optional]

Blend all ingredients together until smooth and serve

Serves 2

NUTRITIONAL INFORMATION PER SERVING:
Calories 296, Fat 7.4g, Saturated fat 2.5g, Carbohydrates 29g,
Fibre 7.5g Protein 26.5g

Bloated?
Sluggish Digestion?
Stressful Lifestyle?

The organic way to regulate your digestion.

WHEY OF LIFE

Breakfast dishes

IT IS TRUE that breakfast is the most important meal of the day and a high-fibre, protein-packed meal is by far the best choice. Many people skip breakfast because of time constraints or just that they don't fancy it or can't be bothered. Whey Protein adds a great dimension to any breakfast and can be whizzed up into a quick smoothie, stirred into porridge or for a more relaxing brunch, fill a protein-packed pancake with fresh, seasonal fruit. Adding Whey Protein to breakfast is a great way to start the day. The satiating effects of protein will keep your blood-sugar levels steady and keep you going until lunchtime.

Protein Power Porridge

High-fibre porridge is known to stabilise blood-sugar levels and provide long-lasting energy. Adding Whey Protein is a simple way to further enhance these benefits.

100 g / 4 oz rolled oats
270 ml / 9 oz water or milk or combination of both
2 scoops Solgar *Whey to Go® Protein Powder* –
Vanilla or any other flavour
1 tsp *Omega Advanced Blend* [optional]
2 tsp xylitol [optional]

Method

● Place the oats and water or milk in a small pan
● Bring to the boil, stirring to encourage the porridge to thicken
● After about 5 minutes or once the porridge is thick, remove from heat and stir in the *Whey to Go® Protein Powder*
● Pour the porridge into bowls and sprinkle with xylitol
● Stir in the *Omega Advanced Blend* oil and serve

Serves 2

NUTRITIONAL INFORMATION PER SERVING:
Calories 298, Fat 10.5g, Saturated fat 0.5g, Carbohydrates 36g, Fibre 5.5g, Protein 21.1g

SOLGAR

Omega

ADVANCED BLEND 2:1:1

A complete Omega 3,6,9 profile in just one teaspoon a day

The Natural and Organic Awards 2008
WINNER
Best New VMS Product

Vegan formula rich in Omega 3, 100 mg plant DHA per teaspoon

———————

Perfect for all ages

———————

An easy way to get your daily Omega 3-6-9

Very Berry Breakfast Pancakes

These gluten-free pancakes, topped with fresh berries and yogurt make a healthy and substantial breakfast. Their fluffy texture makes them great for dessert pancakes too, where they can be topped with frozen yogurt and chocolate shavings or chopped nuts.

Pancakes

150 g / 5 oz brown rice flour
75 g / 3 oz potato flour
2 scoops Solgar *Whey to Go® Protein Powder* – Mixed Berry flavour
1-2 tbsp sugar or xylitol
1 ½ tsp baking powder
½ tsp xantham gum
2 eggs
3 tbsp olive oil
Milk or soy / rice milk alternative – enough to make a thick, pouring batter

Topping

150 g / 6 oz fresh mixed berries
[blueberries, strawberries, raspberries etc]
500 g / 18 oz natural yogurt or soy yogurt
Xylitol for sprinkling on top [optional]

Method

● In a bowl, sift together the rice flour, potato flour, xylitol or sugar, baking powder, whey protein powder and xantham gum

● Stir in eggs, oil and milk and mix until well blended – it's easier to do this using an electric whisk

● Heat a well oiled frying pan over medium-high heat. Spoon pancake mixture into pan and cook until bubbles begin to form [For a thicker fluffier soufflé-like pancake, just add more mix to the pan]. Flip, and continue cooking until golden brown on bottom

Serve immediately with fresh berries and yogurt. Sprinkle with xylitol or add maple syrup, honey or any other topping of your choice

Makes 6 pancakes

NUTRITIONAL INFORMATION PER SERVING:
Calories 410, Fat 13.5g, Saturated fat 2.5g, Carbohydrates 46g, Fibre 3g, Protein 17.3g

Millet, Pear and Apricot Pudding

A tasty gluten-free porridge, combining sweet pears with dried apricots, enriched with *Whey to Go® Protein Powder* to provide a power packed breakfast or delicious snack.

125 g / 5 oz millet
750 ml / 26 fl oz water
2 pears, peeled, cored and chopped
150 ml / 5 fl oz milk or milk alternative eg. soy
50 g / 2 oz cashew nuts
2 scoops Solgar *Whey to Go® Protein Powder* Vanilla flavour
8 dried apricots
1 tsp cinnamon
1 tbsp ground flaxseed

Method

● Put the millet and water in a saucepan and bring to the boil
● Simmer, covered, for about 20 minutes. Add the pear and continue to cook for a further 10 minutes until almost all the water has been absorbed. Set aside
● Place the remaining ingredients in a blender or food processor and process until smooth and creamy
● Pour the nut mixture into the millet and stir well
● Serve hot or cold

Serves 4

NUTRITIONAL INFORMATION PER SERVING:
Calories 311, Fat 10.5g, Saturated fat 2.3g, Carbohydrates 40.1g, Fibre 6.5g, Protein 21.1g

Apple and Blueberry Breakfast Cake

A delicious protein-rich loaf, combining the classic
breakfast ingredients of oats, yogurt, fruit and honey.

150g/ 6oz wholemeal flour
50g/ 2oz oats
2tsp baking powder
3 scoops *Whey to Go® Protein Powder* Mixed Berry flavour
1 Bramley apple
100g/4oz sugar or xylitol
2tbsp honey
300g/12oz natural yogurt
3 eggs
1 tsp vanilla extract
120ml/4fl oz olive oil
75g/3 oz fresh or frozen and defrosted blueberries

Method

● Preheat oven to 180°c/ gas mark 4 and grease and line
a 2lb/900g loaf tin
● Peel and core the apple. Either grate or chop finely in
a food processor. Set aside
● In a large bowl, sift flour, baking powder and Whey
Protein Powder. Stir in oats
● In a separate bowl place oil, sugar (or xylitol), honey,
vanilla extract, eggs and yogurt. Using a whisk, mix
together until well combined
● Add wet ingredients to the dry ingredients and gently mix
until well combined. Fold in the apple
● Pour half the mix into the prepared loaf tin. Sprinkle on
the blueberries and then top with the remaining cake mix
● Bake for 50 – 60 minutes or until an inserted skewer
comes out clean

Continued overleaf

Continued from previous page

Serves approximately 12

NUTRITIONAL INFORMATION PER SERVING:
Calories 214, Fat 10.7g, Saturated fat 2g,
Carbohydrates 17.8g, Fibre 2g, Protein 8.5g

Berry Crunch Pots

An easy-to-assemble crunchy fruit fool – much healthier
than supermarket or cafe versions. Using a range of nuts
and seeds provides essential fats, protein, vitamins and
minerals. Prepare the topping in advance and store in an
airtight container.

Crunchy Topping

25 g / 1 oz macadamia nuts and 25 g / 1 oz cashew nuts
100 g / 4 oz porridge oats
25 g / 1 oz desiccated coconut
1 tbsp ground flaxseed
1 tbsp pumpkin seeds
½ tsp ground cinnamon
1 scoop Solgar *Whey to Go® Protein Powder* Vanilla
or Honey Nut flavour
3 tbsp agave nectar
3 tbsp apple juice
2 tbsp coconut butter, melted or olive oil

Berry Yogurt

250 g / 10 oz natural yogurt

2 scoops Solgar *Whey to Go*® *Protein Powder* –
Mixed Berry flavour

200g / 8oz mixed berries, fresh or frozen

Method

- Place the nuts in a food processor to coarsely chop
- Place the nuts in a bowl with the oats, coconut, seeds, cinnamon and protein powder
- Mix together the agave nectar, apple juice and oil
- Pour over the oat mixture and thoroughly combine
- Spread the mixture out on to a baking tray and toast in the oven at 200°C, gas mark 6 for 10-15 minutes until golden brown
- Stir occasionally during cooking
- Allow to cool. This can be stored in an airtight container until needed
- Place the yogurt, berry protein powder and berries into a blender or food processor and process until smooth and creamy
- Spoon the fruit mixture into four glasses and top with the crunchy oat mixture

Serves 4-6

NUTRITIONAL INFORMATION PER SERVING:
Calories 589, Fat 16.8g, Saturated fat 4.5g, Carbohydrates 107.2g, Fibre 4.9g, Protein 15g

WHEY OF LIFE

Savoury dishes

Here is a selection of savoury dishes which demonstrate the versatility of Whey Protein Powder.

Pan Fried Sea Bass
with Vanilla, Tarragon Sauce

This delicately flavoured fish dish combines tarragon and vanilla in a light creamy sauce. Elegant enough for a dinner party yet speedy enough for when time is short. Instead of sea bass use other white sustainably caught fish such as halibut, cod, haddock or coley. The sauce also works well over grilled mushrooms or poached eggs for a vegetarian option.

4 sustainably caught sea bass fillets, about 100 g [4 oz] each
Olive oil for brushing
1 tbsp olive oil or coconut butter
1 shallot, finely chopped
4 tbsp white wine or vermouth
150 ml / 5 fl oz fish stock or vegetable stock
100 ml / 4 fl oz double cream or soy cream
2 scoops Solgar *Whey to Go® Protein Powder* Vanilla flavour
2 tsp chopped tarragon leaves
Salt and freshly ground black pepper

Method

• Brush both sides of the fish fillets with a little olive oil and season with salt and pepper

• In a pan heat the olive oil or coconut butter. Sauté the shallot for 2-3 minutes until softened. Pour in the white wine, fish stock and cream. Bring to the boil and simmer for 5 minutes to reduce and thicken. Add the protein powder and tarragon. Using a hand-held blender or liquidiser process the sauce until smooth

• Season to taste

• Heat a non-stick frying pan and add a little additional olive oil

Once hot cook the fish, skin side down for 1-2 minutes

Turn over and cook for a further minute until just cooked

• Place the fish fillets on to plates and spoon around the sauce to serve

Serves 4

NUTRITIONAL INFORMATION PER SERVING:
Calories 299, Fat 19 g, Saturated fat 9.2 g, Carbohydrates 1.5 g, Fibre 6.5 g, Protein 19 g

Chicken Wraps with Spicy Mole Sauce

Try this speedy variation of a traditional South American dish. The combination of chilli and chocolate creates a velvety, rich, spicy sauce and the addition of Protein Powder is a simple way to boost the protein value of this dish. Serve with some mixed salad, sliced avocado and lime wedges for a delicious family dish.

1 dried chilli
4 sundried tomatoes
1 tbsp coconut butter or olive oil
1 red onion, chopped
2 garlic cloves, crushed
½ tsp ground cinnamon
½ tsp ground cloves
400 g / 14 oz can chopped tomatoes
2 scoops Solgar *Whey to Go® Protein Powder* – Chocolate flavour
50 g / 2 oz plain dark chocolate, grated
1 tbsp almond nut butter or peanut butter
8 small wholemeal tortillas
3 roasted chicken breasts, sliced
2 tbsp toasted flaked almonds
Handful of fresh coriander leaves, chopped

To Serve
Avocado, soured cream, lime wedges

Method
● Soak the chilli and sundried tomatoes in boiling water for 15 minutes. Drain but reserve the soaking liquid. Deseed the chilli. Chop the chilli and sun dried tomatoes roughly and set aside

• Heat the oil in a frying pan and sauté the onion and garlic until softened, about 2-3 minutes. Add the spices, chilli, sun-dried tomatoes and chopped tomatoes. Add 150 ml / 5 fl oz soaking liquid and simmer gently for 15 minutes until thickened. Place the tomato mixture into a food processor or liquidiser with the Protein Powder, chocolate and nut butter. Process to create a creamy sauce

• Return the sauce to a pan and keep warm. If too thick add a little water. Warm the tortillas according to the packet instructions. Pile the chicken on top, spoon over a little sauce and roll up. Sprinkle over the flaked almonds and chopped coriander. Serve with mixed salad, avocado and lime wedges

Serves 4

NUTRITIONAL INFORMATION PER SERVING:
Calories 451, Fat 19.5g, Saturated fat 5.6g, Carbohydrates 33.9g, Fibre 3.5g, Protein 19.5g

Variations
Spicy Chicken Casserole
Make the sauce as above. Seal chicken pieces in a little oil in a large casserole dish until brown. Pour over the sauce. Bring to a simmer, cover and place in the oven. Cook at 180°c, gas mark 4 for 30-40 minutes until the chicken is cooked through. Add a little stock or water during cooking if it gets too dry. Season to taste. Sprinkle over the flaked almonds and coriander to serve.

Spicy Bean Mole Wraps
For a meat-free option, use a tin of mixed beans or refried beans to replace the chicken.

Spicy Bean Burgers
with Sweet Chilli Dipping Sauce

Turn a bean burger into something special with this protein-packed flavoursome dish. Healthy and filling, this is perfect for kids, family meals and eating al fresco.

2 x 400 g / 14 oz cans cannellini beans, drained and rinsed
½ red pepper, finely chopped
100 g / 4 oz wholemeal breadcrumbs
2 scoops Solgar *Whey to Go® Protein Powder*
Vanilla flavour
1 tbsp no-added-sugar tomato ketchup
1 tbsp chopped fresh coriander
½ tsp cayenne pepper or mild chilli powder
1 egg
Sea salt and freshly ground black pepper to taste
Little olive oil or coconut butter for frying

Dipping Sauce

2 tomatoes, chopped
100 g / 4 oz xylitol
6 tbsp rice wine vinegar
1 red chilli, deseeded, chopped
2 garlic cloves, crushed
1 tbsp lime juice

Method

● Place the beans and pepper into a food processor and pulse on and off to roughly mash. Alternatively use a potato masher to mash the beans then mix in the pepper. Be careful not to over-process. Tip into a large bowl and mix in the breadcrumbs, protein powder, tomato ketchup, coriander, cayenne and egg. Season to taste

- With dampened hands form the mixture into 10-12 burgers. Place on a tray and chill for 30 minutes
- To make the dipping sauce, put all the ingredients into a blender or food processor and process until smooth. Pour into a pan and simmer gently for 5 minutes. Allow to cool and pour into a bowl
- Preheat the grill to high
- Heat a little olive oil or coconut butter in a non-stick frying pan and fry the burgers for 2-3 minutes on each side until crisp and golden. Alternatively place the burgers on a baking tray and brush the top with a little olive oil. Place under a preheated grill and cook for 5-10 minutes on each side until crisp and golden
- Serve with the dipping sauce

Makes 10-12 burgers

NUTRITIONAL INFORMATION PER BURGER
WITH DIPPING SAUCE:
Calories 132, Fat 1.2g, Saturated fat 0.3g, Carbohydrates 28.7g, Fibre 3.2g, Protein 8g

Variations
Vanilla & Lime Yogurt Sauce:
Instead of the dipping sauce blend together the zest of 1 lime and 1 tbsp lime juice, 1 tsp xylitol, ½ scoop vanilla flavour whey protein powder and 200 g natural yogurt. Spoon over the burgers to serve.

Chestnut and Cranberry Stuffing Balls

Much more than an accompaniment to a traditional roast. This meat-free stuffing is full of sweet, fruity flavours, bursting with nutrients and protein. Use it to perk up a Sunday lunch or festive meal.

2 tbsp olive oil or coconut butter
1 red onion, finely chopped
200 g / 8 oz cooked, peeled chestnuts, finely chopped
100 g / 4 oz fresh or frozen cranberries
100 g / 4 oz stale wholemeal bread crumbs
2 scoops Solgar *Whey to Go® Protein Powder*
Mixed Berry or Vanilla flavour
1 tbsp fresh parsley, chopped
Salt and freshly ground pepper
1 medium egg

Method

● Preheat the oven to 200°c, gas mark 6
● Heat 1 tbsp oil in a frying pan. Heat the onion and fry for 2-3 minutes or until soft
● Stir in the chestnuts, cranberries, breadcrumbs, Protein Powder and parsley. Cook for 3-4 minutes until the cranberries have softened
● Season well then transfer to a bowl. Cool slightly
● Add the egg to bind

- Using damp hands roll out the stuffing mixture into about 16-18 walnut-sized balls
- Pour the remaining oil into a large frying pan
- Gently fry the balls in batches until they are lightly coloured, about 3-4 minutes. Arrange them in a single layer on a small non-stick baking tray
- Roast for 10 minutes or until crisp and golden brown

Serves 4-6

NUTRITIONAL INFORMATION PER SERVING [4]:
Calories 326, Fat 5.9g, Saturated fat 1.1g, Carbohydrates 49.4g, Fibre 3.7g, Protein 8.9g

Variations:

Instead of small balls, place the mixture into a greased, shallow ovenproof dish and cook for 20 minutes until crisp and golden.

Serve with a Cranberry, Apple and Orange Chutney:

Place 150g / 6oz cranberries in a pan with 2 chopped and peeled eating apples, 50g / 2oz xylitol, juice of 2 oranges and 2 tsp apple cider vinegar. Simmer for 10-15 minutes until the cranberries and apple are soft and mushy. Stir in 1 scoop of Mixed Berry flavour Whey Protein Powder to increase the protein content. Serve hot or cold. This makes a great accompaniment to cold meats and cheese platters, too.

Apricot & Nut:

Instead of the cranberries add 50g / 2oz dried apricots, finely chopped and 3 tbsp pine nuts. Replace the Mixed Berry Protein Powder with Vanilla or Honey Nut flavour.

Muffins

Muffins are the ultimate tea-time treat.
They don't have to be unhealthy as these
recipes will show. Adding nutritious
ingredients such as Whey Protein, nuts,
seeds and dried fruit can transform
a recipe into a healthy lunch-box snack
or a nutritious breakfast on the run.
You can also experiment with non-wheat
and gluten-free flours. Use these recipes
as a template to create your own favourite
muffins. The possibilities are endless.

Honey Nut Banana Muffins

A sweet nutty muffin, popular with children. Use as part of a breakfast on the run - maybe with an additional piece of fruit.

200 g / 8 oz wholemeal flour
4 tbsp olive oil or melted coconut oil or butter
4 eggs
2 scoops Solgar *Whey to Go® Protein Powder* – Honey Nut flavour
2 large ripe bananas mashed
Few drops vanilla extract.
100 g / 4 oz sugar or xylitol
1 tsp baking powder
50 g / 2 oz chopped pecan nuts
Approx 180 ml / 6 fl oz milk, or milk alternative – enough to make a batter

Method
- Sift flour, Whey Protein Powder and baking powder into a bowl
- Add sugar and vanilla extract
- Add the eggs, oil and milk and beat together to make a soft batter
- Fold in the bananas and pecan nuts
- Fill 12 muffin cases – ¾ full with the muffin mix
- Bake at 190°c / gas mark 5 for 20-25 minutes or until golden brown

Makes 12 Muffins

NUTRITIONAL INFORMATION PER SERVING:
Calories 189, Fat 9.6g, Saturated fat 1.5g, Carbohydrates 18.9g, Fibre 2.9g, Protein 8g

Choc-o-Nut Muffins

A tea-time treat that provides all the rich flavour of a
shop-bought muffin, but using only natural ingredients.

200 g / 8 oz wholemeal flour
1 tsp baking powder
3 scoops Solgar *Whey to Go® Protein Powder* Honey Nut,
or Chocolate or Vanilla flavour
4 eggs beaten
75 g / 3 oz chopped walnuts
100 g / 4 oz brown sugar or xylitol
1 ½ tbsp cocoa powder
2 tbsp dark chocolate chips or grated chocolate
4 tbsp olive oil, melted coconut oil or Pure spread
Approx 7 fl oz / 210 ml milk / rice or soy milk – enough to
make a soft batter

Method

- Sift flour, baking powder and Protein Powder into a bowl.
- Add cocoa and sugar or xylitol
- Add the eggs and olive oil to the dry ingredients and beat
mixture, gradually adding enough milk to make a batter
- Fold in the walnuts and chocolate chips
- Use mixture to fill muffin cases – [fill to just over halfway
as the muffins will rise significantly]
- Cook at 190°c / gas mark 5 for 20 - 25 minutes until well
risen and firm to the touch

Makes 12 Muffins

NUTRITIONAL INFORMATION PER SERVING:
Calories 198, Fat 10.8g, Saturated fat 1.75g, Carbohydrates 16.8g,
Fibre 2.8g, Protein 9.5g

Wheat-Free Cranberry Muffins

A light and fluffy, fruity muffin for those on wheat-and gluten-free diets.

150 g / 5 oz rice flour
50 g / 2 oz potato flour
½ teaspoon xantham gum
1 tsp baking powder
3 scoops Solgar *Whey to Go*® *Protein Powder* – Mixed Berry flavour
100 g / 4 oz sugar or xylitol
1 tbsp ground flaxseeds
3 eggs
4 tbsp olive oil
Few drops vanilla extract
75 g / 3 oz dried cranberries
Approx 150 ml / 5 fl oz milk or milk alternative – enough to make a soft batter

Method

● Sift flours, Whey Protein Powder, xantham gum and baking powder into a bowl
● Add all other ingredients [except cranberries] and beat in enough milk to make a soft batter
● Fold in cranberries
● Fill muffin cases – ¾ full
● Bake at 190°c / gas mark 5 for 25-30 minutes until golden brown

Makes 8-10 muffins

NUTRITIONAL INFORMATION PER SERVING:
Calories 210, Fat 8.5g, Saturated fat 1.6g, Carbohydrates 40.3g, Fibre 2g, Protein 9g

Blueberry Corn Muffins

Golden in colour and bursting with juicy blueberries, these light muffins are a perfect treat for a gluten free/wheat-free diet.

100 g / 4 oz cornmeal
100 g / 4 oz rice flour
1 level tbsp baking powder
½ tsp xantham gum
100 g / 4 oz butter, Pure spread, or coconut butter - melted
1 egg
3 tbsp honey
100 g / 4 oz sugar or xylitol
3 scoops Solgar *Whey to Go® Protein Powder* Berry or Vanilla flavour
180 ml / 6 fl oz milk, or milk alternative
75 g / 3 oz fresh or frozen and defrosted blueberries

Method

● In a large bowl, combine rice flour, cornmeal, baking powder, xantham gum and Whey Protein Powder
● Using an electric mixer, whisk together the melted butter, egg, xylitol, honey and milk
● Using a wooden spoon mix the butter mixture into the dry ingredients until smooth
● Fold in the blueberries
● Spoon mixture into muffin cases and bake at 200°c / gas mark 6 for 20-25 minutes or until the muffins are set and golden brown

Makes 9 Muffins

NUTRITIONAL INFORMATION PER SERVING:
Calories 196, Fat 7.3g, Saturated fat 1.5g, Carbohydrates 24.6g, Fibre 2.1g, Protein 8.3g

Spiced Sweet Potato Muffins

Bursting with healthy carotenoids, these gluten-free, delicately spiced muffins are not only tasty, but with their subtle orange colour, look intriguing too.

1 medium sweet potato
175g/ 7oz rice flour
¾ tbsp baking powder
100g /4oz sugar or xylitol
½ tsp ground cinnamon
½ tsp ground ginger
½ tsp ground nutmeg
180ml/ 6fl oz rice or soya milk
3 scoops Solgar *Whey to Go® Protein Powder*
Vanilla flavour
1 egg – beaten
2 tbsp olive oil

Method

● Preheat oven to 200°c/ gas mark 6. Line a muffin tin with 12 paper cases
● Peel sweet potato and cut into chunks. Steam for 10 minutes, or until very soft
● Place the potato in a food processor and process to a puree
● In a large bowl sift together rice flour, baking powder, xylitol, Whey Protein Powder, and spices
● In a separate bowl mix together rice milk, egg and oil. Stir in the pureed potato until the mixture forms a thick orange liquid
● Fold the potato mixture into the dry ingredients and gently mix until well combined
● Fill 12 muffin cases (just over half full) with the batter
● Bake for 20-25 minutes or until well risen and firm to the touch

Makes 12
Variation:
Use butternut squash or pumpkin instead of sweet potato.

NUTRITIONAL INFORMATION PER SERVING:
Calories 114, Fat 3g, Saturated fat 0.5g,
Carbohydrates 14.7g, Fibre 1g, Protein 6g

Almond Muffins
These gluten-free muffins are so simple to make and show off the versatility of ground almonds. Their mildly nutty, chocolate flavour makes them popular with children and adults alike.

200g/ 8oz ground almonds
2 tsp baking powder
3 scoops Solgar *Whey to Go® Protein Powder*
Chocolate flavour
4oz coconut butter, butter or Pure spread
3 eggs
6 tbsp agave syrup or honey

Method
● Preheat oven to 150°c/ gas mark 3 and line 12 muffin cases
● Mix all dry ingredients together in a bowl
● Combine eggs, honey and melted butter
● Fold egg mixture into dry ingredients and gently mix to form a batter
● Fill each muffin case ½ to ¾ full and bake for 20-25 minutes until well risen and firm to the touch

Makes 12
NUTRITIONAL INFORMATION PER SERVING:
Calories 214, Fat 14.6, Saturated fat 2.2g, Carbohydrates 13.8g,
Fibre 1.6g, Protein 9.1g

WHEY OF LIFE

Flapjacks, Bars and Sweet Treats

Shop-bought flapjacks and bars are often loaded with fats, sugars and other undesirable ingredients. Making your own is easy once you know how and with the addition of protein, fibre and other nutrient-dense ingredients, these treats no longer need to be confined to the occasional indulgence, but rather can be part of your regular, healthy diet.

Apricot and Vanilla Flapjacks

A healthy, high-fibre, not overly sweet flapjack bar for the kids' lunchboxes or great as a mid-morning snack. Add nuts and/or seeds for an even more nutritious bar.

200 g / 8oz oats
100 g / 4oz butter or coconut butter, melted
3 tbsp agave syrup or runny honey
2 tbsp ground flaxseeds
3 scoops Solgar *Whey to Go® Protein Powder* – Vanilla flavour
Few drops vanilla extract
100 g / 4oz chopped dried apricots

Method

● Combine all dry ingredients in a bowl
● Mix the agave syrup with the melted butter and add to the dry ingredients. Add the vanilla extract
● Mix well and then press into a greased baking tray [approx 8" by 8"]
● Bake at 190°c / gas mark 5 for 15 – 20 minutes until toasted brown
● Cut into squares while still warm, then leave to cool before serving

Makes 9 flapjacks

NUTRITIONAL INFORMATION PER SERVING:
Calories 236, Fat 9.4g, Saturated fat 5g, Carbohydrates 19.4g, Fibre 3.9g, Protein 10.1g

Peanut Butter & Chocolate Power Balls

A variation on honey-nut balls for chocolate lovers.

2 tbsp crunchy peanut butter
1 tbsp runny honey
3 scoops Solgar *Whey to Go® Protein Powder* –
Chocolate flavour
1 tbsp ground flaxseeds
1 tbsp *Omega Advanced Blend 2:1:1*
1 tbsp cocoa powder
1-2 tbsp chopped nuts
Apple juice or rice milk – 1-2 tsp
if needed to bind mixture

Method

● Using a metal spoon, combine all ingredients except apple juice and chopped nuts in a bowl
● Work together with your hands to form a firm paste similar to the consistency of marzipan
● Add a few drops of rice milk or apple juice if needed to bind
● Form into 8 small round balls about the size of a walnut
● Roll balls in chopped nuts and refrigerate for 30 minutes

Makes 8 balls

NUTRITIONAL INFORMATION PER SERVING:
Calories 121.6, Fat 7.8g, Saturated fat 1g, Carbohydrates 7.3g,
Fibre 2g, Protein 8.5g

Honey Nut Power Balls

A protein-rich, high-fibre sweet treat that can be made in minutes. Great for lunch boxes or as a post-workout snack for active individuals.

2 tbsp almond butter
1 tbsp runny honey
3 scoops Solgar *Whey to Go® Protein Powder* –
Honey Nut flavour
1 tbsp ground flaxseed
2 tbsp oats
1 tbsp desiccated coconut or ground almonds
1 tbsp *Omega Advanced Blend 2:1:1*
Apple juice or rice milk – 1-2 tsp if needed to bind mixture

Method

● Using a metal spoon, combine all ingredients except apple juice and coconut in a bowl
● Work together with your hands to form a firm paste similar to the consistency of marzipan. Add a few drops of rice milk or apple juice if needed to bind
● Form into 8 small round balls about the size of a walnut
● Roll balls in coconut or ground almonds and refrigerate for 30 minutes

Makes 8 balls

NUTRITIONAL INFORMATION PER SERVING:
Calories 136, Fat 8.3g, Saturated fat 2.5g, Carbohydrates 8.2g,
Fibre 2.2g, Protein 8.5g

Luxury Chocolate Crunchies

A really indulgent treat that adults and kids alike will love. Packed with protein and fibre, these are great for those with a sweet tooth, looking for a healthier snack.

150 g / 5 oz quinoa flakes
50 g / 2 oz oats
100 g / 4 oz butter or coconut butter,
or Pure spread - melted
4 tbsp agave syrup or runny honey
75 g / 3 oz xylitol
2 tbsp ground flaxseeds
3 scoops Solgar *Whey to Go® Protein Powder*
Chocolate flavour
100 g / 4 oz desiccated coconut
2 tbsp cocoa powder
25 g / 1 oz chopped hazelnuts
50 g / 2 oz dark chocolate [at least 70% cocoa solids]

Method

• Mix the melted butter and agave syrup
• Place all the dry ingredients [except the dark chocolate] in a separate bowl
• Add the butter and syrup to the dry ingredients and mix thoroughly
• Press mixture firmly into a well greased baking tray [approx 8"x 8"]
• Cook at 190°c / gas mark 5 for 20 minutes
• Remove from oven and allow to cool for 15 minutes
• Melt the dark chocolate and spread thickly over the baked cake
• Refrigerate to set topping and then cut into squares

Makes 9 [or 16 bite-size]

NUTRITIONAL INFORMATION PER SERVING:
Calories 369, Fat 21.2g, Saturated fat 8.9g, Carbohydrates 27.3g, Fibre 7g, Protein 11.9g

Dark Chocolate Decadence

This gluten-free, flourless cake is truly a chocolate lovers' dream. Served warm with ice cream or frozen yogurt, it also works well as a luxurious dessert that would impress any dinner-party guest.

200 g / 8 oz dark chocolate [at least 70% cocoa solids]
1 tbsp brandy [optional]
125 g / 5 oz xylitol
125 g / 5 oz coconut butter, butter or Pure spread
100 g / 4 oz ground almonds
5 eggs
3 scoops Solgar *Whey to Go® Protein Powder* Chocolate or Vanilla flavour

Method

- Melt the chocolate, xylitol and butter in a bowl – either over a pot of simmering water or in a microwave
- Once melted, remove from the heat and add brandy if using
- Add the ground almonds and Whey Protein Powder to the chocolate mixture and mix well. [Don't worry if the mixture seems a little stiff at this stage.]
- Add the egg yolks one at a time and beat well, setting aside the egg whites in a separate bowl
- Beat the egg whites until stiff, then fold into the chocolate mixture
- Pour into a well greased 9" [23 cm] round cake tin and bake at 180°c / gas mark 4 for 35-45 minutes
- Leave to cool and cut into slices

Serves 12

NUTRITIONAL INFORMATION PER SERVING:
Calories 262, Fat 20.9g, Saturated fat 7g, Carbohydrates 8.8g, Fibre 2.5g, Protein 8g

High-Fibre Muesli Slice

A wholesome bar that can be eaten at breakfast, used as a lunchbox filler or even a tasty dessert. Packed with seeds, this is not only a protein-rich bar, but also high in healthy fats, minerals and fibre.

100 g / 4 oz no-added sugar muesli
50 g / 2 oz oats
25g / 1 oz puffed rice
50 g / 2 oz dried mixed berries – goji, cranberries etc
1 tbsp sesame seeds
1 tbsp mixed sunflower and pumpkin seeds
1 tbsp ground flaxseeds
3 scoops Solgar *Whey to Go® Protein Powder* –
Mixed Berry flavour
100 g / 4 oz melted butter or coconut butter
or Pure spread
4 tbsp agave nectar or honey

Method

- Combine the melted butter and agave nectar
- In a separate bowl, combine all the other ingredients
- Add the butter/syrup to the dry ingredients and mix well
- Press mixture into a well greased shallow tin [approx 8"x 8"]
- Bake at 180°c / gas mark 4 for 20-25 minutes until golden brown
- Leave to cool for 10 minutes, cut into 9 squares and leave to cool completely before serving

Makes 9 slices

NUTRITIONAL INFORMATION PER SERVING:
Calories 253, Fat 10.4g, Saturated fat 2.4g, Carbohydrates 26.5g, Fibre 3.5g, Protein 8.6g

Oatein Bars

Protein bars can be expensive and sometimes contain less than desirable ingredients. These tasty and economical oat bars are packed with only healthy ingredients, as well as being ultra-simple to make.

100g/ 4oz oats
25g/ 1oz oat bran
100g/ 4oz puffed rice
1tbsp pumpkin seeds
100g/ 4oz coconut
4 scoops Solgar *Whey to Go® Protein Powder* –
Chocolate flavour
50g/ 2oz butter
3 tbsp peanut butter
5 tbsp runny honey
2 tbsp *Omega Advanced Blend 2:1:1*

Method

• Place oats, oat bran, puffed rice, coconut and pumpkin seeds in a food processor and blend to a fine meal (about 45 seconds). Turn into a mixing bowl and stir in the Whey Protein Powder
• In a sauce pan melt the peanut butter and honey over a low heat. This can also be done in the microwave if you prefer
• Add the peanut butter mixture and *Omega Advanced Blend* to the bowl of dry ingredients and combine
• Turn the mixture into a shallow baking tray (8" x 8") and press firmly
• Refrigerate for 2-3 hours and then cut into bars

Makes 12

NUTRITIONAL INFORMATION PER SERVING:
Calories 264, Fat 14.4g, Saturated fat 6g, Carbohydrates 27.4g,
Fibre 3.9g, Protein 10g

Almond Cookies

The humble almond is such a versatile nut. Rich in vitamin E, healthy fats, fibre and many other nutrients, they form the basis for these simple, moreish cookies.

100g/4oz ground almonds
2tbsp melted Pure spread or coconut butter
3 tbsp runny honey or agave syrup
3 scoops Solgar *Whey to Go® Protein Powder* Chocolate flavour
1 tsp vanilla extract
1 tbsp desiccated coconut
¼ tsp baking powder

- Preheat oven to 150°c/ gas mark 3 and line a baking tray with greaseproof (parchment) paper
- Combine all dry ingredient in a bowl
- Stir in the melted butter and honey
- Using wet hands, form the mixture into eight walnut sized balls and place, well spaced, on a lined baking sheet
- Flatten each ball and prick with a fork
- Bake for 12-15 minutes until slightly risen
- Remove from oven and place on a wire cooling rack

Makes 8

NUTRITIONAL INFORMATION PER SERVING:
Calories 176, Fat 11g, Saturated fat 3.9g, Carbohydrates 12.5g, Fibre 2.1g. Protein 9g

// If you want to live a healthy and active life, drink whey and dine early. //

FLORENCE, ITALY, CIRCA 1650

// If everyone was raised on whey, doctors would be bankrupt. //

ITALY, CIRCA 1777

WHEY OF LIFE

Desserts

The dessert recipes here are just as lavish as any good dessert should be. Packed with protein and healthy carbohydrates, they'll keep your blood sugar levels balanced and leave you comfortably satisfied at the end of your meal.

Strawberry and Vanilla Cheesecake

A delicious wheat-free cheesecake – creamy yet low in sugar and rich in protein. Adding Protein Powder to the base and filling is a fantastic way of boosting your protein intake without increasing unnecessary fat and calories. Simple to make, too – it takes minimum effort but tastes like you've spent hours in the kitchen.

Base

150 g / 6 oz plain fine oat cakes
1 ½ scoops Solgar *Whey to Go® Protein Powder* Vanilla or Honey Nut flavour
100 g / 4 oz butter, melted
2 tbsp agave nectar

Filling

3 eggs, free range, beaten
4 tbsp xylitol
450 g /1lb ricotta cheese
2 tbsp corn flour
2 scoops Solgar *Whey to Go® Protein Powder* Vanilla flavour
Few drops of natural vanilla extract
Zest and juice of 2 lemons
100 g / 4oz strawberries

Decorate

100 g / 4 oz strawberry pure fruit spread
150 g / 6 oz strawberries, sliced

Method
- Preheat the oven to 200°c / gas mark 6
- Place the oat cakes in a food processor and process to form fine crumbs
- Add the Protein Powder, butter and agave and combine thoroughly
- Spoon the mixture into a greased, spring form loose bottomed 23 cm [9 inch] round cake tin, and press down with the back of a spoon
- Bake in the oven for 10 minutes
- Place the filling ingredients in a food processor and blend until smooth
- Pour into the prepared crust
- Bake for 10 minutes then reduce the heat to 150°c gas mark 3 and cook for a further 30 minutes until firm and lightly golden
- Allow to cool in the tin
- Warm the fruit spread in a pan gently
- Spoon over the cheesecake and top with the strawberries
- Chill for a further 30 minutes before serving

Serves 8

NUTRITIONAL INFORMATION PER SERVING:
Calories 539, Fat 23.8g, Saturated fat 13.2g, Carbohydrates 89.4g, Fibre 0.8g, Protein 17.6g

Variations:
Strawberry and Lemon
Omit the vanilla extract and add the zest of 2 more lemons to the filling.

Chocolate Base:
For a subtle chocolate flavour – replace the Vanilla Protein Powder with chocolate flavour instead.

Chocolate Avocado Pots

Rich and velvety – this little pot of chocolate is the perfect way to finish off a meal. A truly luscious dessert – full of nutritious ingredients, rich in protein yet low in sugar. It may seem odd but chocolate and avocado creates a winning combination.

75 g / 3 oz pitted dates, soaked in boiling water
3-4 tbsp agave nectar to taste
2 small avocados, peeled, pitted and chopped
2 scoops Solgar *Whey to Go® Protein Powder*
Chocolate flavour
50 g / 2 oz plain dark chocolate [75% cocoa solids], melted
Little apple juice to thin if necessary

To decorate:
2 tbsp grated dark chocolate 75% cocoa solids

Method
• Drain the dates and place in a food processor with the rest of the ingredients
• Process until smooth and creamy. Add a little apple juice to thin the mousse if necessary
• Spoon the mousse into ramekins and decorate with the grated chocolate

Serves 6

NUTRITIONAL INFORMATION PER SERVING:
Calories 620, Fat 6.3g, Saturated fat 2.6g, Carbohydrates 152g, Fibre 2g, Protein 6.5g

Variation:
Instead of dates try prunes. For a special occasion soak the prunes in a little Armagnac and top with chopped pistachio nuts.

Fruity Yogurt Cups

This super healthy, ultra simple dessert has no limits.
It can be made with any fruit of your choice, fresh, frozen
or why not try stewed fruits on a cold winter's day.
Delicious topped with seeds, nuts or granola.

2 peaches or nectarines
125 g / 5 oz raspberries
1 kiwi fruit

Topping

250 g / 10 oz live natural yogurt
2 scoops Solgar *Whey to Go® Protein Powder* Vanilla,
Berry, Honey Nut or Chocolate flavour

Method

● Cut the fruit into pieces and divide between two glasses
or small bowls
● In a separate bowl, stir the yogurt and
Whey Protein Powder together
● Top the fruit with the yogurt mix
● If you wish, top with seeds or chopped nuts

Serves 2

NUTRITIONAL INFORMATION PER SERVING:
Calories 290 Fat 6.25g, Saturated fat 3.75g,
Carbohydrates 37.g, Fibre 6g, Protein 25g

Chocolate Buckwheat Waffles

A delicious gluten-free dessert, waffles make a fantastic base for all kinds of adventurous toppings. These chocolate waffles are great served with fresh strawberries, bananas or any other fruit – and of course, a generous helping of maple syrup.

150 g / 6 oz buckwheat flour
50 g / 2 oz rice flour
2 tbsp oil or melted butter, Pure spread or coconut butter
3 scoops Solgar *Whey to Go® Protein Powder* Chocolate or Vanilla flavour
2 eggs
300 ml / 10 fl oz milk or milk alternative
1½ tsp baking powder
100 g / 4 oz sugar or xylitol
25 g / 1 oz cocoa powder

Method

- Whisk the eggs until they are pale and frothy
- Whisk in the milk and melted butter or oil
- Place all dry ingredients into a bowl
- Add the liquid ingredients and beat with a wooden spoon to form a smooth batter
- Ladle into a waffle iron and cook for 3 minutes or according to the manufacturer's instructions
- Top with fresh fruit or any topping of your choice

Makes 8-10 waffles

NUTRITIONAL INFORMATION PER SERVING:
Calories 154, Fat 5.7g, Saturated fat 1.2g, Carbohydrates 19.4g, Fibre 2.6g, Protein 10g

Variation:

Omit the cocoa powder and use an alternative flavour Whey Protein Powder and other compatible ingredients. For example, use Honey Nut Whey Protein and add chopped nuts to the waffle mix before cooking.

About the author

Alice Bradshaw D.N. MED

Alice Bradshaw studied at The College of Nutritional Medicine, now known as Plaskett International.

At the age of 23 she joined SOLGAR VITAMINS, where she could express her passion for natural health as well as further her knowledge in this area. In her early years at Solgar, she gained a diploma in Sports Nutrition. She works as Solgar's Education Manager in the Technical Department assisting consumers, practitioners and other health professionals with diet-and health-related queries. Alice also provides material for health writers and journalists and her quotes and articles have been featured in various national publications, including *Natural Products News*, *Health Food Business*, *Women's Fitness*, *Health and Fitness*, *Men's Health*, *The Daily Mirror*, *Netdoctor.co.uk*, *FHM* and *Bella Magazine*.

Contributor

Christine Bailey MSc PGCE
Qualified nutritional therapist, Food and Health Writer, Advisor, Chef and Cookery / Health Trainer.

Well known in the Health and Food Industry, Christine assists companies on product development, recipes and promotional material, presenting at shows and events and running cookery demonstrations and workshops.

Christine has more than a decade of experience in the food and health sector, writing for numerous health and food magazines, newspapers and working on local radio. Magazines Y*ou Are What You Eat*, *Optimum Nutrition*, *Natural Health and Beauty*, *Here's Health*, *Allergy Magazine*, *Natural Lifestyle*, *Organic Life*, *Pregnancy*, *Prima Baby*, *Mother and Baby*, ASDA *Good For You* as well as many food, health and family websites and charities including the World Cancer Research Fund UK. Christine is also an author of several health and recipe books.

// Thank you for showing me a way of getting a healthy breakfast into my 10 and 13 year old boys. **They love the smoothies** and even enjoy making them for themselves, giving me a few more precious moments under the duvet. //

PATRICIA, 42
HOUSEWIFE AND MUM OF TWO

// Having recently been advised by my nutritionist to avoid wheat, I have been **inspired** by this recipe book to experiment with wheat-free ingredients to create tasty and healthy treats that my **whole family** can enjoy. //

MADELEINE, 37
DENTAL NURSE